ELEMENTARY GEOLOGY FOR CHILDREN

AF601848

ELEMENTARY GEOLOGY FOR CHILDREN

G.S. RAMAKRISHNARAO
B.Sc. (Hons.) (GEOLOGY); M.Sc. (ORE DRSSING);
M.S. (METALLURGY) (M.I.T, USA)

Published by Zorba Books, November 2022
Website: www.zorbabooks.com
Email: info@zorbabooks.com
Author Name : G.S. RAMAKRISHNARAO
Copyright ©: G.S. RAMAKRISHNARAO

Title: ELEMENTARY GEOLOGY FOR CHILDREN

Printbook ISBN: 978-93-95217-02-6
Ebook ISBN: 978-93-95217-03-3

All rights reserved. No part of this book may be reproduced or transmitted in any form or by any means, electronic or mechanical, except by a reviewer. The reviewer may quote brief passages, with attribution, in a review to be printed in a magazine, newspaper, or on the Web—without permission in writing from the copyright owner.
The publisher under the guidance and direction of the author has published the contents in this book, and the publisher takes no responsibility for the contents, its accuracy, completeness, any inconsistencies, or the statements made. The contents of the book do not reflect the opinion of the publisher or the editor. The publisher and editor shall not be liable for any errors, omissions, or the reliability of the contents of the book.
Any perceived slight against any person/s, place or organization is purely unintentional.

Zorba Books Pvt. Ltd. (opc)
Sushant Arcade,
Next to Courtyard Marriot,
Sushant Lok 1, Gurgaon – 122009, India

Printed by Thomson Press (India) Ltd.
B-315, Okhla Industrial Area, Phase 1, New Delhi- 110020

In memory of my beloved wife,
Gundimeda Radha Devi
Who initiated my Graduate Study at M.I.T; Cambridge, USA
in September 1957

Contents

Foreword

I am N Sandhya Devi, daughter of G.S. RamakrishnaRao who is the author of this book entitled **"ELEMENTARY GEOLOGY FOR CHILDREN"**. I am delighted to write the foreword. During his era, the only courses for a stable career were either medicine or engineering subjects. Today, in the digital age of computer and artificial intelligence, career option in Information technology is highly sought after as it is lucrative with early settlement.

This is undermining the option of choosing a career in arts and sciences, commerce & economics, architecture, law, etc. When children do not have the aptitude or opportunity to undertake professional courses or cannot pursue due to parent's financial constraints, alternative careers are considered.

Nature is a mystery and everything reflected in it cannot be explained. Global warming is happening. All of us have heard and felt earthquakes but not the tsunami, until it happened, nobody heard of forest fires or high temperatures in Europe, rising sea levels in the pacific, save Soil movement etc. What are these and why are they happening? Parents are at a loss when questioned on these aspects. Geography may explain but geology, physical and applied will give more information.

I have presumed, that my dad is a well-known geologist and metallurgist. It still perplexes me as to how in the 1950's, from a small-town background, how did a school headmasters son know, that a career in geology can be taken up and what will be the lifestyle thereafter. The journey is interesting. After completion of MS in MIT Boston, USA, he came back to India and started as a Scientist in NML, Jamshedpur, previously Bihar and presently Jharkhand in the 60's. Then he moved to Delhi worked in NMDC, developed the Research and development lab of NMDC in Hyderabad Telangana in 1972. He was in charge of Bababudan iron ore project, Chikmagalur Karnataka in 1978, associated with other iron ore projects at Kirandul, Bailadila, Donimalai and Kudermukh. He was the General manager of R&D, labs, NMDC, Hyderabad, till retirement in 1992. He kept himself engaged post retirement, till the age of 80 years as a consultant to UNIDO and later MSPL Hospet and is healthy and fit at 87. Simply put, he has garnered rich experience of 50 years of service in mineral engineering field, generating revenue from rock, hills and mountains, producing iron from low/ high grade iron ore for steel production, generation of diamonds etc. He has authored many research publications, classified, when in service. He has also authored the book "Mineral processing techniques" "Basics and related issues" based on hands on experience, for students pursuing ore dressing applied geology mining and metallurgy published by Zorba publishers. The next latest contribution was written during the pandemic.

Life of geologists, metallurgists, mining engineers in central government organizations, is a breeze. Memories indicate, collection of colorful rocks in various shapes and sizes, "the specimens", for what not understood, visits to R&D, Geological survey of India, trekking, lots of travelling through innumerable serpentine narrow roads to hill stations in jeep, vans, projects, seeing greenery and brownery and razing of hillock and mountains, reforestation, lifestyle shock, transfers, moms support at home and during construction of the house. A childhood, full of adventure, enjoyment, imbibing values and how to be self-sufficient.

I have reviewed the book and added the photographs of rock collections and the book is for a geology pursuant. The book answers some questions on earthquakes volcanoes ores etc and is a good read for one and all.

Chapter I

Mother Earth

Once, a doctor couple were moving around a museum. The husband suggested to his wife, let us skip the geology section dealing with useless information about rocks and minerals. But the wife insisted on going through the section closely as it was her brother, a geologist, who persuaded her to study medicine and in turn, she wanted to move around quickly to get a bird's eye view of the subject. Finally, they mutually agreed to get a basic idea of geology.

While growing up, every child asks their parents, at some time or another, inquisitive questions such as the following:

1. Will the waterfall not take a break?
2. Why do earthquakes occur?
3. What is there deep in the earth? Does the moon & other planets contain water, air, or rocks?
4. Do we get water if a well is dug in our back yard?
5. When will the active volcano in Indonesia or Alaska erupt next?
6. Why does the sea level rise at Mumbai shoreline, submerging adjacent land?
7. Can we find gold in our farmhouse?
8. Why is the Sahara in Africa "a desert"?
9. Why are the glaciers melting?
10. How do we get hot water springs in Yellowstone National Park in Wyoming?

Knowledge of geology may help parents to answer questions from children.

As you know, mother earth contains practically all the elements we need. The elements are unevenly distributed including precious elements like gold, silver, platinum; iron ore, limestone, dolomite, quartz for making iron and steel; strategic elements required for producing alloys; fuels for meeting energy requirements etc.

But these elements and minerals are not uniformly distributed throughout the earth.

Much below the earth's surface, there are molten rocks called magma, which contain different elements at very high pressure and temperature.

Due to various geological processes such as weathering by streams, rivers, and seas, geothermal activities, tectonic movements cause earthquakes, volcanos, and pegmatites etc. There is a higher concentration of the desired mineral in some localities/regions compared to other areas.

Due to uneven distribution, groundwater-geologist detects and finds its precise location.

A petroleum geologist locates oil and gas fields.

Atomic minerals are located by an atomic scientist using Geiger muller counter.

Minerals are also hidden deep underneath our earth. Several probes are being sent by different countries to explore and find the nature of minerals and rocks hidden in outer planets and satellites such as the Moon and Mars.

Geologists find the precise location of various minerals present in the mother earth, estimate the concenteration of the desired element found in an ore body, localize the element, mark the boundary, identify the reserves and associated waste/gangue minerals. The findings are reported to the geological society or appropriate agency for assessing its technoeconomic feasibility and publicizes them for taking financial/investment decisions.

Chapter II

Physical Geology

Geology is the study of our earth. It is based on the following fields of sciences:

Physics and Chemistry to understand the geology of the earth.

Geochemistry to understand the chemistry of earth's interior, distribution of elements, minerals and rocks on the surface of the earth.

Geophysics to predict the occurrence of minerals, earthquakes, volcanoes, tsunamis and underground water.

Physical geology to understand weathering process by seas, rivers, streams and wind.

Mineralogy and crystallography to identify minerals and rocks, their composition and their crystal structure.

Broadly, the earth has three zones:

The atmosphere contains air and other gasses that we breathe in.

The hydrosphere includes oceans, seas, rivers, lakes, wells etc.

Biosphere deals with life and living things.

Physical geology includes a study of:

Weathering and erosion of igneous, sedimentary, and metamorphic rocks.

TABLE I: CLASSIFICATION OF ROCKS AND MINERALS

Rock type	Origin	Route	Composition & minerals	Environment	Examples of minerals formed
Igneous rocks	Formed due to solidification of molten magma coming out of earth's interior at very high temperature and high pressure	Passes through all cracks/different tectonic layers/weak zones	Has the original chemical & mineral composition of magma as well as that of the host rocks	Solidifies on cooling in proper environment	Apatite Diamond Calcite Quartz, Magnetite, Ilmenite
Sedimentary rocks	Formed due to weathering of igneous or metamorphic rocks	By stream/river/wind/ physical/chemical decay of exposed rocks. They move from their original position to some other location.	Essentially retains the original rock composition	Formed over long periods of time	Limestone, placer gold, diamonds Bauxite, Coal, Laterite
Metamorphic rocks	Formed out of the preexisting igneous or sedimentary rocks	On exposure to very high temperature and pressure deep in the interior of earth			Quartz, feldspars, micas, pyroxene, garnet, kyanite, talc

Igneous rocks are formed due to the solidification of molten magma and include granites and basalt.

Sedimentary rocks are formed due to weathering of igneous and metamorphic rocks and include sandstone, limestone, coal, and shale.

Metamorphic rocks are formed from igneous and sedimentary rocks on being subjected to extremely high temperature and pressures. eg. Marble, slate.

Earth movements include earthquakes frequently occurring in certain zones such as Japan and other countries. They involve sudden movement of land mass causing immense destruction of life and property. Recently, in June 2020, residents of Gujarat, Rajasthan, Delhi (India) experienced several low-intensity earthquakes. Afghanistan experienced an earthquake in June 2022 with a death toll of over 1000 persons.

Mountain building: The Himalayas, Rocky Mountains and Grand Canyon of Colorado, Andes mountains, and Alps are examples.

Isostacy phenomena explains the reason for co-existence of the tallest mountains such as the Himalayas and deepest oceans such as the Pacific Ocean and the plateau such as Tibet.

When volcanoes erupt, the molten rocks called magma comes out from the earth's interior with gases at extremely high temperature and pressure. The magma provides valuable information about the interior of the earth. In June 2020, there was a volcanic eruption in Indonesia.

Continental drifts: Huge continental land masses are drifting extremely slowly across the oceans and colliding against each other.

Tectonics: Earth's lithosphere consisting of several tectonic plates are moving extremely slowly over billions of years.

Folds: Occur due to severe stresses, twists and bends in the rock masses.

Faults: Break in large rock mass along which a part of it moves against the other in a rough plane.

Origin of oceans, seas, lakes, hot water springs, waterfalls (Niagara waterfalls), Glaciers.

Natural fuels including graphite, coals, and petroleum.

Underground water, Oil and gas fields.

Deserts such as Sahara deserts, Egyptian sand sea, Death Valley, California etc.

Wet and dry seasons such as Mozambique, Tanganyika, Nigeria etc.

As our young readers see, geology is one of the most exciting fields of science, worth exploring after you grow up. The primary object of this book is to create an interest in geology in children and young adults. But at such a young age as you are, children should not be burdened with more details nor facts and figures.

Microscopes are used for identification of gangue and ore minerals

Like every individual has specific features, every mineral has a particular identification characteristic like crystal structure, color, streak, hardness, specific gravity, magnetic property, cleavage, mineral association etc. A geologist identifies most of these minerals based on his experience on his field trips. However, he confirms his findings based on his laboratory study on a microscope.

Gangue is the rocky material associated with the ore that needs to be removed to get pure ore.

The basic characteristics of useful minerals are presented in table II.

TABLE II: BASIC CHARACTERISTIS OF USEFUL MINERALS

MINERAL	COMPOSITION & % OF CHIEF ELEMENT/ METAL	SP.GR	H	CRYSTAL	COLOUR	ORE SOUGHT FOR
Apatite	$Ca_5(PO_4)_3(F, Cl)$ P_2O_5: 42%	3.1-3.3	4-5	hexagonal	green	Phosphate
Barite	$BaSO_4BaO$: 65.7%	4.3-4.6	3	rhombohedral	white yellow	Barium
Bauxite	$Al_2O_3,3H_2O$ AL: 35%	1-3		amorphous	white, brown	Aluminum ore
Biotite	Mica mineral	2.7-3.0	2.5-3	monoclinic	black, brown	Mica
Calcite	$CaCO_3$. CaO;56%	2.7	3	hexagonal	white, yellow	Calcium
Cassiterite	SnO_2 Sn: 79%	7	6-7	tetrahedral	brown or black	Tin ore
Chalcopyrite	$CuFeS_2$. Cu;34.6	4.2	3.5 - 4	tetrahedral	brass to gold yellow	Copper
Chromite	$FeOCr_2O_3$. Cr: 46.2	4.4	5.5	cubic	black	Chromium
Cinabar	HgS	8-8.2	2-2.5		reddish	Mercury
Cobaltite	CoAsS Co: 35.5	5.6-6.3	5-6	cubic	silver white	Cobalt

MINERAL	COMPOSITION & % OF CHIEF ELEMENT/ METAL	SP.GR	H	CRYSTAL	COLOUR	ORE SOUGHT FOR
Columbite	$(Fe,Mn)(Nb,Ta)_2O_6$; Ta_2O_5: VARIABLE	5.3-7.3	4.6	rhomb	brown to black	Strategic mineral
Chalcocite	Cu_2S; Cu: 80%	5.5-5.8	2.5-3			Copper ore
Copper	Cu Cu: 100	8.8	2.5-3	cubic	red	Copper
Corundum, Ruby, Saphire	Al_2O_3 Al: 52.9	4.0-4.1	9	hexagonal	red, yellow, blue	abrasive, precious/ ornamental stones
Cuprite	Cu_2O Cu: 88	6	3.5-4	cubic	red	Copper
Diamond	C C: 100	3.1-3.5	10	cubic	white, yellow, red, vary with inclusions	Ornaments
Feldspar	Silicate mineral					Porcelain
Dolomite	$CaCO_3$ $MgCO_3$ MgO: 21.4	2.8-3	3.5-4.5	hexagonal	white, yellow	Steel making

MINERAL	COMPOSITION & % OF CHIEF ELEMENT/ METAL	SP.GR	H	CRYSTAL	COLOUR	ORE SOUGHT FOR
Fluorite/ Fluorspar	CaF_2 F: 48.9	3-3.3	4	Cubic	yellow, blue	Flourite
Galena	PbS; Pb;86.6	7.5	2.5	cubic	gray	Lead
Garnet	$Mg_3Al_2(SiO_4)_3$					Some used as precious stones
Gold/native gold	Au; Au: 100	14 -19.6	2.5-3	cubic	yellow	Gold;
Graphite	C; C: 100%	2.2	1-2			Electrodes
Gypsum	$CaSO_4,2H_2O$ CaO: 32.6	2.3	1.5-2			Cement
Hematite	F_2O_3 Fe: 70%; becomes magnetic upon heating in reducing conditions	4.9-5.3	5.5-6.5	hexagonal	gray/black/ reddish	Iron
Ilmenite	$FeOTiO_2$ Ti: 31.6 Magnetic	4.4-4.9	4.5-6	hexagonal	brown, black	Strategic/paints
Limestone (Marble)	$CaCO_3$; Ca: 40 %;					Widely used
Magnesite	$MgCO_3$; Mg: 28.9;	3-3.2	3.5-4.5	hexagonal	white, yellow	Refractories, strategic

MINERAL	COMPOSITION & % OF CHIEF ELEMENT/ METAL	SP.GR	H	CRYSTAL	COLOUR	ORE SOUGHT FOR
Magnetite	Fe_3O_4; Fe: 72.4% Magnetic	5-5.2	5.5-6.5	cubic	black	Iron
Mercury	Hg: 100					Liquid metal
Molybdenum	MoS_2	4.7-4.8	1-1.5	hexagonal	gray	Strategic
Monazite	$(CeLaDi)PO_4$, TH SI O4 THORIUM: 9%	5.2-5.3	5-5.5	monoclinic	red/yellow	Strategic
Platinum	PT; PT: 100%; sometimes magnetic with gold	13 -19	4.6	cubic	silver	Ornament
Pyrite	FeS_2	5.8	6-6.5	cubic	brass to gold yellow	Associated with gold, copper,
Pyrolusite	MnO_2; Mn: 63.2	4.7-4.9	2-2.5	Rhombohedral	black, gray	Manganese
Psilomelane	MnO_2H_20 K_2BaO_2					Manganese
Pyrrhotite/ magnetic pyrite	Fe_2S_4	4.5-4.7	3.5-4.5	Hexagonal	yellow, red	Nickel
Quartz	SiO_2	2.6	7	Hexagonal	different colors	Building

MINERAL	COMPOSITION & % OF CHIEF ELEMENT/ METAL	SP.GR	H	CRYSTAL	COLOUR	ORE SOUGHT FOR
Rhodochrosite	$MnC0_3$	3.3-3.8	3.5-4.5	Hexagonal	red, pink	Manganese
Rutile	TiO_2; TI: 60%	4.3-5.1	6-6.5	Tetrahedral	reddish, brown	Strategic, Paints
Scheelite;	$CaWO_4$; W: 63.9	8.5-9.6	4.5-5	Tetrahedral	white, yellow	Tungsten ore
Siderite	$FeCO_3$	3-3.9	3.5-4.5	Rhobohedral	black, gray	Iron
Sillimanite	$Al_2O_3SiO_2$	3.25	6-7.5	Rhombohedral	gray, brown	Abrasive
Silver	AG; AG: 100	10-11	2.5-3	Cubic	white to grey	Ornament
Sphalerite	ZnS; Zn: 67%	3.9-4.1	3.5-4	Cubic	white, yellow	Zinc ore
Sulphur	S	2.	1.5-2.5	Rhombohedral	yellow	Multiple uses
Talc	$3MgO_4SiO_2H_2O$-silicate mineral	2.7-2.8	1-1.5	Monoclinic	white, gray	Cosmetics
Tantalite	Tantalum ore	6.5-8.2	6	Rhombohedral	black, reddish	Strategic
Tourmaline	Iron, Mg Mn mineral	2.9-3.2	7-7.5	Hexagonal	black, brown	Ornament

MINERAL	COMPOSITION & % OF CHIEF ELEMENT/ METAL	SP.GR	H	CRYSTAL	COLOUR	ORE SOUGHT FOR
Uraninite Pitch blende	Uranium bearing mineral	6.5-9.7	5.5	Cubic or amorphus	gray, brown, black	Atomic miineral
Wolframite	(Fe Mn)WO_4 W:51.3	7.2-7.5	5-5.5			Tungsten strategic mineral
Zircon	Zr Si O_4 ; Zr O_2: 67.2	4-4.8	7.5	Tetrahedral	yellow, grey, green	Multi uses

The Moh's hardness scale, which indicates the relative hardness of a particular mineral in comparison with the hardest diamond, is presented in TABLE III.

TABLE III: MOH'S HARDNESS SCALE

Hardness	Reference mineral
1	TALC
2	GYPSUM
3	CALCITE
4	FLUORSPAR
5	APATITE
6	FELDSPAR
7	QUARTZ
8	T0PAZ
9	CORUNDUM
10	DIAMOND

TABLE IV: CRYSTAL FORMS – BASIC FEATURES

"A CRYSTAL CAN BA DEFINED AS A POLYHEDRAL SOLID BOUNDED BY A PLANE OF SURFACES WHICH EXPRESS AN ORDERLY INTERNAL ARRANGEMENT OF ATOMS AND MOLECULES"

SYSTEM	CRYSTAL NAME	AXES DESIGNATION AND NATURE OF AXES	TYPE OF SURFACES	EQUALITY OF FACES	TYPICAL MINERALS
I	CUBIC	a,a,a. THE THREE AXES ARE OF EQUAL LENGTHS WHICH INTERSECT AT RIGHT ANGLES TO EACH OTHER	ALL SURFACES ARE PERPENDICULAR TO EACH OTHER	EQUAL	GALENA, PYRITE, FLUORSPAR, MAGNETITE, PYRITE
II	TETRAGONAL	a,a,c, IT HAS THREE MUTUALLY PERPENDICULAR AXES. HORIZONTAL AXES ARE EQUAL & THE THIRD VERTICAL AXIS IS EITHER SHORTER OR LONGER THAN THE REST.	FOUR FACED SOLID. EACH FACE IS AN EQUILATERAL TRIANGLE & MEETS THE AXES AT EQUAL DISTANCE.		ZIRCON, RUTILE, CASSITERITE, ZINC BLENDE

SYSTEM	CRYSTAL NAME	AXES DESIGNATION AND NATURE OF AXES	TYPE OF SURFACES	EQUALITY OF FACES	TYPICAL MINERALS
III	HEXAGONAL	a,a,a,c, THREE EQUAL LENGTH AXES ARE IN A HORIZONTAL PLANE INTERSECTING AT 120 ^{0} WITH EACH OTHER. VERTICAL AXIS IS AT RIGHT ANGLES TO THE PLANE CONTAINING THE HORIZONTAL AXES.		UNEQUAL	BERYL, CALCITE, QUARTZ, TOURMALINE, APATITE
IV	ORTHORHOMBIC	a,b,c ALL THE THREE AXES ARE UNEQUAL BUT AT RIGHT ANGLES TO EACH OTHER			BARITES, SULPHUR, COLUMBITE
V	MONOCLINIC	a,b,c ALL THE THREE AXES ARE UNEQUAL.TWO OF THEM ARE IN A PLANE AND INTERSECT AT ACUTE OR OBTUSE ANGLE. THE THIRD AXIS IS PERPENDICULAR TO THE PLANE INCLUDING THE OTHER TWO.	THE PLANE INCLUDING THE OTHER TWO		GYPSUM, TALC
VI	TRICLINIC	a,b,c; ITS THREE UNEQUAL AXES INTERSECT AT ACUTE AND OBTUSE ANGLES.			AXINITE

TABLE V: UNIQUE CHARACTERISTICS OF SOME MINERALS

SPECIFIC CHARACTERISTIC	MINERAL NAME .1	MINERAL NAME .2	MINERAL NAME .3	MINERAL NAME .4	MINERAL NAME .5	MINERAL NAME .6	MINERAL NAME .7
Highly magnetic	Magnetite						
Moderately magnetic	Ilmenite	Pyrrhotite Only magnetic sulfide mineral					
Magnetic on heating in reducing atmosphere	Hematite						
Magnetic on heating	Siderite						
Feebly magnetic	Franklinite Sometimes magnetic	Platinum Sometimes magnetic					
High specific gravity >7	Cinnabar 8 -8.2	Native copper 8.8	Galena 7.4-7.6	Gold 15.6-19.3	Platinum 17	Silver 10.5	Uraninite 9-9.7
Higher hardness >7	Andalusite 7.5	Beryl 7.5-8	Corundum, ruby, 9	Diamond 10 Found sometimes with magnetic gold	Spinel 8.0	Wolframite 7.2-7.5	Zircon 7.5

Gangue mineral like quartz, feldspar, mica, calcite is studied in the transmitted light under a polarizing microscope. Thin sections of these minerals are prepared to make them suitable for identification.

Ore minerals like galena, chalcopyrite, pyrite, sphalerite, magnetite, hematite are opaque. They are unsuitable for study under transmitted light in a polarizing microscope. So highly polished specimens of these minerals are prepared for identification in an ore microscope under reflected light.

The geologist identifies the mineral, the association of ore and gangue, the extent of their abundance, estimates the grade, reserves and whether it is worth mining the ore.

Chapter III

Minerals for Ornamental Use

III.1: Silver minerals

Occurs in nature in a pure state

Silver ores:

- Native silver (Ag): Ag: 100%.
- Associated minerals: Gold, copper.
- Argentite (Ag_2S); Ag: 87%.
- Associated minerals: cobalt, nickel.
- Some siliceous ores contain silver.

Silver is recovered during smelting of other associated metalliferous sulfide ores such as copper, lead, zinc, etc.

Occurrence occurs in contact with metamorphic zones, hydrothermal veins, and replacement deposits.

Silver is the most malleable and ductile element.

It is a good conductor of heat and electricity.

Native silver: Mexico, Nevada, Broken hills (N.S.W)

Argentite: Colorado, Gem stock lode of Nevada.

Uses: Silver is used for the manufacture of ornaments, coins, alloys etc.

Major production centers: Mexico, USA, Canada, Russia, Peru.

III.2: Gold

Gold is not evenly distributed on mother earth. It is concentrated in specific isolated zones.

Composition: Native gold (pure): 100% Au

It occurs in combination with tellurides or refractory ores (possibly as selenides)

Auriferous sulfides and pyrite.

Gold is malleable and ductile. It does not tarnish.

Occurrence: occurs in quartz veins and placer deposits.

It occurs in a free state in alluvial deposits. In a few areas, gold can be recovered just by panning.

But it occurs mostly with silver, copper, and mercury as a gold amalgam.

In India, gold was mined from a deep underground mine at Kolar gold fields, but the mining was stopped around 1960 when the operations became highly unsafe and uneconomical.

Presently, it is mined on a smaller scale at Hutti gold fields. Gold is recovered as a by product from smelter of the copper concentrator, Ghastlie, Bihar, Khatri, Rajasthan. etc.

A new gold deposit was found in Bihar recently. Reserves of gold, techno-economic feasibility and other related issues are being evaluated.

Uses: It is used by almost all governments for holding as an asset in treasuries. It controls the world economy.

It is used for coinage.

It is also used for ornamental purposes.

Gold can be used as security for taking loans, easy sales, it is used as an asset value.

Major producers: Free gold associated with pyrites is available at Kalgoorlie (Western Australia), Colorado, Ontario.

III.3: Diamond

Composition: Carbon (C)

It is essentially a carbon mineral (C: 100%) but contains small inclusions.

Crystal structure: Cubic

Color: White, yellow, red, green, blue. Inherent impurities alter the original color.

Luster: Transparent.

Fracture: Conchoidal

Hardness: 10

Specific gravity: 3.5

Occurrence:

i. Occurs in ultra-basic igneous rocks ex: Kimberly mine. They are mined in south Africa, Russia, Brazil, New South Wales, Australia, etc.
ii. It also occurs in alluvial deposits. Ex: West Africa, Brazil, India (Panna, M.P). Found in placers with gold.

Uses: Primarily for ornaments, gems, abrasive purposes

The value of a diamond depends on its size, brilliance, purity (free from internal inclusions), fire, shape, cut etc.

Major producers of diamonds in the world:

- South and southwest Africa
- Russia
- Ghana
- Congo
- Brazil
- India

III.4: Platinum

Occurs as native platinum: Pt (Chemically pure 100% Pt)

Crystal structure: Cubic

Sometimes, platinum is magnetic when associated with gold.

Color: White

Streak: Grey

Luster: Metallic/opaque

Malleable and ductile

Acid proof

H: 4-5

Sp.gr: 21.5

Occurrence: Found in basic and ultra-basic igneous rocks, quartz veins, copper deposits and placer deposits

Uses:

- Jewelry
- Dentistry
- Electrical trade
- Chemical industry

Major producers: Russia, S. Africa, Canada.

III.5: Garnet
(pyrope and almandite –partly precious)

Garnets are silicates of various divalent and trivalent metals having the following composition:

1. Pyrope: $Mg_3Al_2(SiO_4)_3$
2. Almandite: $Fe_3Al_2(SiO_4)_3$
3. Grossularite: $Ca_3Al_2(SiO_4)_3$
4. Spessartite: $Mn_3Al_2(SiO_4)_3$
5. Andradite: $Ca_3Fe_2(SiO_4)_3$
6. Varulite: $Ca_3Cr_2(SiO_4)_3$

Pyrope: In part precious garnet.

Crystal system: Cubic

Color: Crimson

Luster: Vitreous

Fracture: Conchoidal

H: 7.5

Sp.gr: 3.7

Occurrence: Ultra-basic igneous rocks in Sri Lanka.

Almandite: In part, precious garnet.

Crystal Structure: cubic

Color: Crimson deep red

Luster: Vitreous

Fracture: Uneven

H: 6.5 -7.5

Sp.gr: 4

Occurrence: Common in metamorphic rocks, mica schists, gneisses and granites

Major producer: Sri Lanka

III.6: Topaz

Composition: $Al_2(F,OH)_2SiO_4$

Crystal structure: Orthorhombic

Cleavage: Perfect

Color: Yellow; pink

Streak: Colorless

Luster: Vitreous

Fracture: Uneven

H: 8

Sp.gr: 3.5

Occurrence: In acid igneous rocks such as granites and contact zones in Colorado

Uses: Gemstone

Production centers: Urals, Brazil, Japan, Rhodesia

III.7: Tourmaline

Composition: Complex boron silicate of aluminum with alkali metals or magnesium

Crystal structure: Hexagonal

Color: Black

Streak: Colorless

Luster: Vitreous

Fracture: Uneven/brittle

H: 7–7.5

Sp.gr: 3–3.2

Occurrence: Granites, pegmatite

Varieties: Red, pink varieties are cut and used as gems

Honey yellow color occurs in Sri Lanka

Use: Some are used as a gemstone

Major production centers: Brazil, Russia, USA, Madagascar

III.8: Amethyst

Composition: Corundum; ruby (Al_2O_3); Al: 52.9%

System: Hexagonal

Cleavage: None

Color: Grey, reddish, greenish, purple

Luster: Vitreous

Fracture: Uneven

H: 9

Sp.gr: 4

Occurrence:

1. Contact metamorphism of shales
2. Crystalline gemstones occur either in limestone or in alluvial deposits as round pebbles.

Uses: Colored varieties are used as gemstones, and abrasives.

Production centers: USA, Canada, India, Rangoon, Rhodesia, S. Africa, Russia

Chapter IV

Nonferrous Ore Minerals

IV.1: Copper minerals

Copper minerals and their composition:

Native copper: Cu; 100% Cu

Cuprite: Cu_2O; Cu: 88.8

Chalcopyrite: $CuFeS_2$; Cu: 34.6; occurs with pyrite and galena

Chalcocite: Cu_2S; Cu: 80%

Covellite: CuS; Cu: 66.5%

Occurrence:

Native copper occurs in the Lake Superior region (USA); Monte Catenin (Italy)

Cuprite: Cheesy (France); Chile (Peru)

Chalcopyrite: Cornwall (Norway); Ghatsila (Bihar, India)

It associates with pyrite, galena, sphalerite.

Chalcocite occurs in Cornwall, Siberia; Mexico; Peru

Uses: Used chiefly as an electrical conductor, alloys.

IV.2: Zinc minerals

Sphalerite: ZnS; Zn: 67%

Zincite: ZnO; Zn: 80.3%

Sphalerite:

Associates with galena and chalcopyrite.

Crystal structure: Cubic

Cleavage: Perfect

Color: Black or brown

Streak: White to reddish

Luster: Resinous

Fracture: Conchoidal

H: 3.5 – 4

Sp.gr: 4

Occurrence:

In association with galena.

Common metasomatic deposits in limestone as in Tri-state (USA).

Hydrothermal lode/vein deposits in Broken hills, (NSW)

Colorado, Cornwall, New Mexico

Uses: Important ore of Zinc

IV.3: Lead minerals

Chief ores of lead:

Galena: PbS; Pb: 86.6%

Anglesite: $PbSO_4$: 68.3

Cerussite: $PBCO_3$; Pb: 79%

Galena:

Crystal structure: Cubic.

Color: Lead grey

H: 2.5.

Sp.gr: 7.5.

Luster: Metallic.

Lead ores are usually associated with silver.

Uses:

To make accumulators

Lead smelting

In making alloys

Chief producers: USA; Russia; Germany.

India produces lead and zinc in small quantities.

IV.4: Aluminum minerals

Main minerals: Corundum (Al_2O_3); Al: 52.9%

Spinel ($MgAl_2O_4$)

Diaspore ($Al_2O_3H_2O$): Al_2O_3: 85%

Gibbsite $Al(OH)_3$; Al: 34.6%

Bauxite (mixture of Al hydroxides); Al; 35%

Bauxite deposits are quite extensive.

Corundum: Dealt with in an earlier chapter.

Bauxite:

Crystal form: Amorphous

Color: White/grey/brown

Occurrence: Weathering of aluminum bearing rocks.

Use: Source of aluminum

Major producers: France, Russia, USA, India, Australia.

IV.5: Tin mineral

Tin ore

Chief mineral: Cassiterite (SnO_2); contains 78.6 % Sn

Bright white metal; malleable and ductile.

Sp.gr: 7.3

Crystal structure: Tetragonal

Color: Black or brown

Occurrence: Normally associated with granites

Lode deposit

Alluvial deposit

Uses: Used in making alloys

Leading producers: Malaysia, China, Thailand, Russia.

IV.6: Nickel minerals

Nickel ores:

Millerite: NiS; Ni: 64.8%

Pentlandite: (FeNi)S; Ni: 22%

Niccolite: NiAs; Ni: 44%; As: 56%

Millerite:

Crystal structure: Hexagonal

Cleavage: Perfect

Color: Brass yellow

Streak: Green

Luster: Metallic

H: 3.5

Sp.gr: 5.5

Occurrence: Associated with iron stone, cobalt

As nodules in south Wales,

As veins in Cornwall, Pennsylvania (USA)

Pentlandite

Crystal structure: cubic

Massive

Color: Yellow

Streak: Black

Luster: Metallic

Fracture: uneven

H: 3.5 -4

Sp.gr: 5

Associated minerals: chalcopyrite, pyrrhotite

Major producer: Ontario, Canada

Use: chief ore of nickel

IV.7: Tungsten minerals

Main minerals:

Wolframite: (FeMn)WO_4; W: 51.3

Scheelite: $CaWO_4$; W: 63.9

Wolframite:

Crystal structure: monoclinic

Cleavage: Perfect

Color: Brown/black

Streak: Brown

Luster: Submetallic

H: 5-5.5

Sp.gr: 7.5

Occurrence:

With granites

Alluvial deposits

Uses:

Production of ferrotungsten alloys for making tool steels

Special alloys

Tungsten carbide for cutting tools

Electric filaments

Chief producers: China, Russia, Korea, USA.

Scheelite: $CaWO_4$

Crystal structure: Tetragonal

Cleavage: Good

Color: yellow, white

Streak: White

Luster: Vitreous

H: 5-5.5

Sp.gr: 6.0

Occurrence: Pneumatolytic origin

Chief uses: Production of ferrotungsten alloys,

Tungsten carbide

Special alloys

Major production centers: Cumberland, Cornwall

Arizona, Connecticut, California, USA

IV.8: Chromium ores

Chromium ore

Chromite: $FeOCr_2O_3$; Cr: 46.2

Crystal structure: Cubic

Color: Black.

Streak: Brown

Luster: Submetallic

H: 5.5;

Sp.gr: 4.5 – 4.8

Occurrence: Ultrabasic igneous rocks, gabbro

Uses: Source of chromium element.

Chief producers of ore: Russia, S. Africa, Rhodesia, Philippines

IV.9: Titanium ores

Titanium minerals:

Rutile: TiO_2; Ti 60%

Ilmenite: $FeTiO_3$; Ti: 31.6%

Ilmenite is magnetic

Minerals associated with ilmenite: pyrite, feldspar

Rutile:

Crystal system: tetragonal

Cleavage: Poor

Color: Red/brown

Streak: Brown

Luster: Metallic

Fracture: Uneven: 6 -6.5

Sp.gr: 4.2

Occurrence: Associated in igneous rocks with granites and their metamorphic components (gneisses).

Beach sands

Uses: source of titanium

Major commercial centers: Virginia; Canada; Australia, Florida, India etc.

Ilmenite:

Crystal system: Hexagonal

Color: Black

Streak: Black/brown

Luster: Submetallic

Fracture: Conchoidal

H: 5 to 6

Sp.gr: 4.5 to 5

Occurrence: Basic igneous rocks and gabbro.

Uses: Source of titanium

Commercial production centers: Norway, Quebec, USA, India, Australia, Florida.

IV.10: Magnesium minerals

Manganese minerals:

Pyrolusite: MnO_2;; Mn: 63.2%

Psilomelane: $MnO_2H_2O.K_2BaO_2$

Rhodochrosite: $MnCO_3$; Mn: 61.7%

Rhodonite: $MnSiO_4$

Braunite: Mn_2O_3

Pyrolusite:

Crystal form: Orthorhombic/pseudomorphs

Color: Grey

Streak: Black

Luster: Metallic/submetallic

Fracture: Brittle

Occurrence:

Sedimentary oxides

Alteration of manganese bearing sedimentary origin rocks

Uses: Important ore of manganese.

Major producers: Russia, Congo, China, S. Africa, Brazil, India

Psilomelane: Hydrated manganese ore with or without Ba and K

Crystal structure: Monoclinic

Form: Massive

Color: Iron black

Streak: Brownish black

Luster: Submetallic

H: 5-6

Sp.gr: 3.7- 4.5

IV.11: Vanadium minerals

Vanadium ore

Vanadium ore: Patronize VSO_4.

Ore mineral: Vanadinite: $(PbCl)Pb_4(VO_4)_3$; metal content is variable.

Though widespread, constituents are found in igneous and metamorphic rocks, large deposits are rare. But vanadium is a bye product of uranium, lead, and zinc ores.

The ore is associated with nickel and molybdenum sulfides.

Uses:

Making ferrovanadium alloys.

Useful to produce very strong tools of steels and special steels.

It is mined in Peru and USA.

IV.12: Molybdenum ore

Molybdenum ore

Ore: Molybdenite: MoS_2; Mo: 60 %

Molybdite: MoO_3; Mo: 66-67%

Crystal structure: Hexagonal

Cleavage: Basal

Color: Lead grey

Streak: Black

Luster: Metallic

Sp.gr: 4.7

H: 1 -1.5

Occurrence: Acid igneous rocks such as granites and pegmatites and contact metamorphic rocks.

Use: Chief ore of molybdenum

Chief producers of molybdenite: USA; Russia, Chile, China, India

IV.13: Magnesium minerals

Chief minerals: Magnesite $MgCO_3$; Mg: 28.9%

Dolomite $MgCa(CO_3)_2$; CaO: 30.4%; Mg O: 21.9%

Magnesite:

Crystal structure: hexagonal

Cleavage: Perfect

Color: White

Luster: Vitreous

Fracture: Conchoidal

H: 3.5 -4.5

Sp.gr: 3

Occurrence: In serpentine masses like in India

Replacement of dolomite and limestone (Austrian deposits)

Uses: for making refractory bricks, furnace linings, crucibles.

Major producers: Manchuria, Quebec, Washington

Dolomite: CaO: 30.4%; MgO: 21.9%

Crystal structure: Hexagonal

Cleavage: Perfect

Color: White

Luster: Opaque

Fracture: Brittle

H: 3.5-4

Sp.gr: 2.8

Occurrence: Alteration of limestones

Deposited from seawater

Uses: Building material

For making refractory linings

Commercial availability: At many geological horizons

IV.14: Cobalt ore

Cobalt minerals

Cobaltite: CoAsS; Co: 35.5%

Crystal structure: Cubic

Color: Silver

Streak: Grey

Luster: Metallic

H: 5.5

Sp.gr: 6-6.3

Occurrence: Found in metasomatic contact deposit, calcite, barite, quartz

Use: Important ore of cobalt

Producers: Ontario, Congo, Zambia, Canada, Germany.

IV.15: Mercury ore

Mercury minerals: (Hg)

Amalgam: Native amalgam: Hg_xAg_y

Cinnabar: HgS

Calomel: Hg_2Cl_2

Native mercury: (quicksilver); Hg; 100%

Liquid metal

Color: White

Luster: Metallic/opaque

Sp.gr: 13.6

occurrence: Found in Italy and Spain. It is a deposit from hot springs.

Cinnabar:

Crystal form: Hexagonal.

Cleavage: Perfect

Color: Red/brownish

Streak: Scarlet

Luster: Dull

Fracture: Uneven

H: 2-2.5

Sp.gr: 8.1

Occurrence: Result of volcanic activity.

Deposited in certain hot springs of volcanic origin.

Occurs in gold –quartz veins.

Uses: Meets the mercury needs.

Important areas of occurrence: Spain. Italy, western USA, Russia

IV.16: Sulphur ores

Sulphur minerals

Native Sulphur: S

Pyrites: FeS_2; Fe: 46.7%

Native Sulphur:

Crystal form: Orthorhombic

Cleavage: Imperfect

Color: Yellow

Streak: Yellow

Luster: Resinous

H: 1.5 – 2.5

Sp.gr: 2

Occurrence: Volcanic origin

Uses:

For the manufacture of sulphuric acid, firecrackers, gun powder, insecticides

Major producers in the world: Japan, England, California, Utah , USA

Pyrites: Also useful as a source of iron.

Usually associated with copper, gold, silver

Mainly used for the manufacture of sulphuric acid

IV.17: Calcite/limestone/marble

Composition: $CaCO_3$

Occurs extensively

Calcite: CaO: 56%

Limestone: Ca: 40%

Calcite: Used in many industries like glass, iron and steel making, paper, soap, paints, cement.

Chapter V

Ferrous Ore Minerals

Chief ore minerals:

Magnetite: Fe_3O_4; 72.4% Fe

Hematite: $Fe_2O_{3;}$ 70% Fe

Goethite: $Fe_2O_3H_2O$

limonite: $2Fe_2O_3 3H_2O$; Fe: 59.9%

Arsenopyrite: FeAsS

Pyrrhotite: FeS; magnetic pyrite

V.1: Magnetite ore

Magnetite: Contains up to 72.4% Fe

Strongly magnetic.

Crystal structure: Cubic

Cleavage: Poor

Color: Black

Streak: Black

Luster: Metallic or submetallic

Fracture: Sub conchoidal

H: 5.5-6.5

Sp.gr: 5.2

Occurrence: Igneous and metamorphic rocks.

Associated minerals: Varied

Major producers in the world: Kiruna (Sweden); USA.

Uses of the ore: Production of iron and steel

V.2: Hematite ore

Hematite: Up to 70% Fe

Becomes magnetic upon heating under reducing conditions.

Crystal structure: Hexagonal

Cleavage: Poor

Color: Steel grey

Streak: Red

Luster: Metallic

Fracture: Uneven

H: 6.5

Sp.gr: 5

Occurrence: Mostly replaces limestone

Use: Production of iron and steel

Associated minerals: Varied

Major producers: Lake Superior (USA)

Brazil (metamorphic ore)

Cuba

Bailadia (India)

V.3: Goethite

Goethite: Up to 62.9% Fe

Crystal form: Orthorhombic

Cleavage: Good

Color: Brown

Streak: Brown

Luster: Adamantine/opaque

H: 5-5.5

Sp.gr: 4-4.5

Occurrence: Associated with hematite and limonite

Use: Source of iron ore

Major producers in the world: Cornwall, Russiac, Michigan (USA)

V.4: Limonite

Comp: Hydrous ferric oxide; 2 $Fe_2O_3.3H_2O$.

Contains up to Fe: 59.9%

Radiating fibrous Structure

Color: Brown

Streak: Brown

Luster: sub metallic.

H: 5 – 5.5

Sp.gr: 4

Occurrence: Mostly altered to other iron oxides.

Use: Source of iron

Major production centers: Spain, Cuba, Sweden, England.

Chapter VI

Strategic Ore Minerals

V1.1: Pitch blende (Uraninite)

Chief strategic minerals:

Pitch blende: Uraninite: UO_2

Radium

Monazite

V1.1: Pitch blende (Uraninite: UO_2)

Crystal structure: Cubic

Color: Black

Streak: Black

Luster: Submetallic/opaque

H: 5-5.5

Sp.gr: 6.4

Occurrence: Igneous rocks, granites, pegmatites

Uses: For cancer treatment and used in nuclear reactors for atomic fission.

Major producers: USA, Canada, Russia, S. Africa etc.

VI.2: Radium

Radium is produced due to the disintegration of Uraninite

Sp.gr: 18.7

These minerals carry U_3O_8 content with varying contents of radium.

Major producers: China, Russia, Korea, USA.

VI.3: Monazite

Composition: It is a phosphate mineral of rare earth metals $(CeLaDy)Po_4ThSiO_4$ with thoria and silica.

Associated minerals: Gold, chromite, and ilmenite

Thorium content: 9%

Crystal structure: Monoclinic

Cleavage: Imperfect

Color: Pale yellow

Streak: White

Luster: Resinous

Fracture: Uneven

H: 5.5

Sp.gr: 5.3

Occurrence: In acid igneous rocks such as granite (pegmatites)

Monazite is found in igneous rocks.

Occurs as a part of seashore sands.

Use: Source of thorium- strategic requirement

Associated minerals: Gold, chromite, iron ore

Major production centers:

Brazil

India (Kerala, Visakhapatnam)

Sri Lanka

Nigeria

Malaysia

Chapter VII

Minerals for Use as Fuels

VII.1: Graphite

Composition: C

Usually contaminated with silica and iron oxides.

Crystal structure: Hexagonal

Color: Iron grey

Streak: Shining black

Luster: Metallic

H: 1-2

Sp.gr: 2 – 2.3

Good conductor of heat

Occurrence: Veins, bedded masses, and in contact with igneous rocks.

Igneous rocks. Ex: Sri Lanka, eastern Canada, India etc.

Specific character: Resembles molybdenite except in its streak.

Uses: Foundry, paints, crucibles, electrodes, lubricants.

VII.2: Coals

They consist of carbon, oxygen, and hydrogen.

They are derived from decomposed vegetation/forest trees after chemical changes over a long period of geological time. They become richer in carbon content with time.

Classification of coals:

Based on carbon content:

Coal type	% carbon content
Peat:	> 50 %
Lignite	> 70 %
Bituminous coals	> 80 %
Anthracite	> 90%

Coals are also classified on the basis of other parameters too:

A. Fuel ratio: Fixed carbon/volatile matter
B. Calorific value is based on its ability to produce heat on burning.
C. Carbon content, volatile matter, and moisture content.
D. Nature of quality coke producible out of coals.

Anthracite:

Anthracite: Contains up to 95 % carbon.

Color: Black

Streak: Black. It does not soil the fingers.

Luster: Brilliant

Fracture: Uneven

H: 0.5 – 2.5

Sp.gr: 1 - 1.8

Gives out relatively much more heat on burning.

Occurrence: South Wales (Scotland), Pennsylvania.

VII.3: Crude petroleum, naphtha, mineral oils

These are produced by fractional distillation of crude petroleum producing various oils such as ether, spirit, benzene, lubricating oils, fuel oils etc.

Petroleum is used chiefly by the automobile industry.

Petroleum is found in the folds and domes of sand stones and dolomites.

These are found in the tertiary age strata. They are of organic origin derived from the long decay of organic matter.

Occurence: Persian Gulf area, Texas, California, USA, Canada, Russia, India etc.

The presence of petroleum is detected by the presence of oil, pitch, and bitumen in its surrounding areas.

Chapter VIII

Silicate Minerals used in Industry

Silicate family includes quartz, feldspathoids, nepheline, leucite etc. Unlike precious elements, non-ferrous, ferrous minerals, strategic minerals, fuels etc. the silicate minerals are widely distributed across the earth.

The chemical composition of common silicate minerals is given in table VI.

TABLE V1: CHEMICAL COMPOSITION OF A FEW COMMON SILICATE MINERALS

MINERAL	COMPOSITION	% METAL	% AL_2O_3
Quartz	SiO_2	46.9 Si	
Albite	$NaAl\ Si_3O_8$		19.5
Analcite	$NaAlSi_2O_6.2\ H_2O$		
Andalusite	$Al_2Si\ O_5$		63.2
Anorthite	$CaAl_2Si_2O_6$		36.7
Orthoclase	$KAlSi_3O_8$		18.4
Microcline	$KAlSi_3O_8$		
Anorthoclase	$(Na,k)AlSi_3O_8$		
Leucite	$KAlSi_2O_8$		
Nepheline	$(Na,K)(Al_3Si)_2O_4$		

Talc	Magnesium bearing silicate	Mg: 19.2	
Zircon	$ZrSiO_4$	Zro_2: 67.2	
Muscovite	$K_2Al_2Si_3O_{19}(OH)_2$		
Biotite	$K(Mg,Fe)_2AlSi_2O_{19}(OH)_2$		
Hornblende	$C_a4Na_2(Mg,Fe)_8(Al,Fe,Ti)_6Si_{12}O_{44}(OH)$		

These silicates, found widely, are used in different industries.

Quartz: Building material, glass industry, optical works etc.

Amethyst, garnet, topaz, tourmaline as gemstones.

Kaolin: For pottery making.

Clay: For making bricks.

Mica: Used as an insulator in electrical industries.

Talc: Rubber industry, filler by paper industry.

Aluminum silicates by refractory industry.

VIII.1: Quartz

Composition: SiO_2

Crystal structure: tetrahedron

Occurrence:

Main constituent of igneous rocks such as granites.

It is called sandstones, quartz in sedimentary formations

It is also found in metamorphic rocks.

Uses: As building material, glass industry, as an abrasive material, pottery, making bricks, in making short wave radio

VIII.2: Feldspars and feldspathoids

Feldspar family

They are the dominant group of igneous rocks.

They are the silicates of potassium, sodium, calcium, or barium. They are listed below:

Orthoclase: $K(AlSi_3O_8)$ or Potassium aluminum silicate.

Albite: $Na(AlSi_3O_8)$ or sodium aluminum silicate

Anorthite: $Ca(Al_2Si_2O_8)$ or calcium Aluminum silicate

General characteristics of orthoclase:

Color: Whitish, grey

H: 6

Sp. Gr: 2.5 – 3

Crystalline system: Monoclinic system

Albite, anorthite in triclinic system.

Feldspars have two principal cleavages.

Uses: Used in porcelain and pottery, sanitary ware, bricks industries etc.

VIII.3: Amphiboles family

Hornblende is the chief mineral of amphibole family.

Asbestos, widely used till recently until it was banned, is the fibrous form of amphiboles family.

Hornblende

They are present in different crystal systems:

1. Orthorhombic amphibole
2. Monoclinic amphiboles
3. Hornblende series

Structure: Monoclinic

Color: Green to black

H: 5-6

Sp.gr: 3-3.5

Alkali amphibole series

Asbestos: It includes fibrous form of amphiboles. The fibers are long, flexible and can easily be separated by fingers.

Use: Making asbestos sheets, both plain and corrugated.

VIII.4: Pyroxene family

They are silicates having the Si_2O_6 chain structure with iron, magnesium, calcium, and aluminum as main components.

Augite is the main mineral.

Crystal form: Monoclinic

Color: Dark green to black

H: 5-6

Sp.gr: 3.8

VIII.5. Talc

Crystal form: Monoclinic

Color: White/grey

H: 1.0 (softest mineral)

Sp.gr: 2.7-2.8

Uses: Rubber industry, filler in paper industry.

VIII.6: Muscovite mica

Composition:

Muscovite: Potassium mica.

Biotite: Iron and magnesium mica or black mica.

Phlogopite: Magnesium mica.

They have perfect basal cleavage that helps in their splitting into thin sheets. Muscovite is mostly used in the electrical industry.

Occurrence of muscovite:

Muscovites are primarily found in igneous rocks, pegmatites, granites as well as gneiss and mica schists of metamorphic rocks.

Chief producers of muscovite: India, Russia, USA, Canada etc.

Uses: As an insulator in the electrical industry.

VIII.7: Biotite

Occurrence of biotite: Biotite is found in igneous rocks, as well as in metamorphic rocks as biotite gneisses and biotite schists. It is called black mica.

Crystal form: Monoclinic

Color: Black/brown/green

H: 2.5-3

Sp.gr: 2.7-3.1

VIII.8: Aluminum silicates

Aluminum silicates family

Chemical composition Al_2SiO_5:

They include:

Andalusite: $Al_2 SiO_5$; Al_2O_3: 63.2

Sillimanite: Al_2SiO_5: Al_2O_3: 63.2

Kyanite: $Al_2 SiO_5$: Al_2O_3: 63.2

They occur in metamorphic rocks. They have clay as the chief ingredient.

Besides refractories, they are used in the porcelain industry and making spark plugs.

Occurrence: Singhbhum district (India), California and eastern part of the USA and South Africa.

Chapter IX

Minerals for Industrial Use

IX.1: Fluorite/Fluorspar Fluorides

Hydrofluoric acid: HF_2

Fluorspar: CaF_2; F: 48.9%

Cryolite: Na_3AlF_6

Apatite: calcium fluoride and phosphate

Apatite: $Ca_3(F,Cl,OH)(PO_4)_3$: P_2o_5: 42%;

Common in metamorphic rocks.

Fluorspar

Crystal form: Cubic

Cleavage: Perfect

Color: Colorless/green/blue etc.

Streak: White

Luster: Vitreous

Fracture: Conchoidal/brittle

H: 4

Sp.gr: 3- 3.25

Occurrence: Hydrothermal veins, replacement deposits associated with galena, quartz, barytes

Chief producing countries: Mexico, USA, Russia, China, Britain

Uses: Enameling, production of hydrofluoric acid, steel making etc.

IX.2: Gypsum

Composition: $CaSO_4.2H_2O$; CaO: 32.6%

Crystal system: Monoclinic

Cleavage: Perfect

Color: Colorless

H: 1.5 – 2

Sp.gr: 2.3

Occurrence: in three ways:

1. Saline residue as in Germany, USA,
2. Limestone
3. Calcium sulphate

Uses: Important mineral for production of cement, fertilizers, filler, paint, rubber etc.

Major producers: USA, Canada, Britain, France

IX.3: Zircon

Composition: $ZrSiO_4$; ZrO_2: 67.2%

Crystal system: Tetragonal

Cleavage: Perfect

Color: Colorless

Streak: Colorless

Luster: Opaque

Fracture: Conchoidal

H: 7.5

Sp.gr: 4.7

Occurrence: in more acid igneous rocks like granite, nepheline-syenite, in some metamorphic rocks and sedimentary beach sands.

Commercial production centers: Madagascar, Brazil, India, Sri Lanka, Australia, Florida.

Uses:

Gemstones

IX.4: Barytes

Composition: $BaSO_4$

Crystal structure: Orthorhombic

Cleavage: Poor

Color: White

Streak: White

Luster: Vitreous

Fracture: Uneven

H: 3.5

Sp.gr: 4.3

Occurrence: Associated with lead and zinc veins as worked in USA. North England, USA

Production centers: USA, Germany, Canada, Russia, Brazil, India etc.

Uses: Paints, wallpaper, drilling mud, asbestos goods.

IX.5: Beryl

Chief mineral

Beryl: $Be_3Al_2(SiO_3)_6$: Be: 5%

Crystal form: Hexagonal

Color: Green/black

H: 7.5-8

Sp.gr: 2.6-2.9

Ore occurrence: Pegmatite veins, gneiss, schist

Associated minerals: Mica, feldspars

Uses: Nuclear reactors, alloys

Chapter X

Reduction of Fossil Fuels & Green Gas Discharges

We use coal in steam engines; coke for iron and steel making as well as for smelting ores for getting precious metals; petrol, and diesel for running our automobiles, trains, ships, and airplanes.

In the process, undesirable poisonous green gasses like carbon dioxide, carbon monoxide, Sulphur dioxide are emitted into the surroundings/air/atmosphere creating unimaginable miseries permanently to the present and future generations. These excessive green gasses increase the atmospheric temperature by about 1.5 to 2°C up to 48°C or more to unbearable levels in some areas causing major disasters like:

Melting of glaciers rise sea levels and submerge areas by about 1.77 feet (0.54 meters) such as in 12 Indian cities like Bombay, Visakhapatnam by about the year 2100 (as per NASA report).

Excessive rains, floods, landslides.

Heat waves causing forest fires, deserts due to the burning of trees.

Volcanoes, earthquakes, tornadoes (common in some western countries), tsunami (caused by very severe earthquakes occurring in deep sea) etc.

As human beings, let us do whatever little we can do to reduce the green gases by adopting the following simple measures:

Switch off the lights, fans, air conditioners, and vehicle engines whenever they are not required, like signal lights.

Let us walk, cycle and use stairs for our heart's good health.

Let us not burn trash, dry leaves, and throw lighted matches into the grass.

Let everyone in the world, including adults and children, understand the urgent need to reduce green gas emissions for human survival and also flora and fauna, including wild animals from today instead of tomorrow.

Let us reduce using coal, coke for thermal generation.

Instead, let us use hydropower, nuclear energy as well as renewable energy from sources like wind and solar power.

Instead of using high-end petrol and diesel engine cars and running them at high speed, which emit excessive green gasses like carbon dioxide, let us use vehicles run on batteries and electricity. Major companies are spending huge amounts of their own resources on developing and producing renewable energy as well as battery storage for running cycles, scooters, cars, and even small planes etc. Solar, wind and tidal energy produced by renewable sources must be utilized irrespective of the fact it may be marginally costlier or cheaper as compared to conventional sources like thermal energy. This will lead to a reduction of green gasses and a better and healthier environment.

Let us consider using solar or wind energy generators to cut down our power bills, if at all it is feasible on the terrace of our houses.

Wherever we are, let us reduce green gases for our own survival.

Chapter XI

Suggestions for Children-Budding Geologists

Whenever you go out on vacation with your parents or friends, carry the following simple items in your haversack bag to identify rocks or minerals you see, and collect them:

1. A small magnet to identify minerals having magnetic properties like magnetite, ilmenite and pyrrhotite.
2. A magnifying glass for identifying cleavages, like pages in a closed book, in the specimen such as asbestos, mica. You can also observe the grain size.
3. A small bottle of dilute hydrochloric acid to identify carbonaceous minerals like limestone, dolomite, magnesite, and marble.
4. A small glass piece to check the relative hardness of the specimen with glass (H: 7). Are you able to scratch the specimen or not with the glass? If you can scratch the specimen, glass is harder than the specimen. Or else the specimen is harder than glass.
5. A small hammer to break the rock and collect a small chip or specimen of it to have for your own "rock museum". When you return to your school/ graduating school, get your findings confirmed by your class teacher or concerned geologist/elders.

Go ahead and have fun learning geology, and collecting colorful stones and be a leader!!!!!

An interesting note by Raghav Venkat Iyer, Student at The Aga Khan Academy, Hyderabad

Being an outdoor person, I naturally developed a bond with rocks. When I was about 8 years old, I bought my first book on rocks and minerals. This book helped me learn more about rocks, its properties and how they look like. After reading the book, I felt that I should start finding some interesting rocks.

My first rock was a sandstone which I collected when I visited Jordan. I was very fascinated by its texture and color. With the help of some educational kits, I learnt to identify the rocks which I had collected. One day when I was casually observing my mother's necklace, I found that each of the stone was shiny, colourful and well rounded.

So, I wondered how a rock which had sharp edges could become that smooth. I immediately checked with an expert about how rocks were polished. Then I found out that a machine called a 'rock tumbler' which was half filled with water and rocks was spun around for days, making them smooth. I was very interested in the process, so when I came of age, I purchased a rock tumbler to learn the secret behind polishing. Just looking at the polished rocks gives me a lot of pleasure, unlocking the beauty within.

"Rocks are big,
To find them you have to dig!
Our best friends they can be,
They are all where we can see!
Rocks are made into road tar!
They can be bigger than a car!"
I dream to be a "rock"star one day.

Collection of 20 Rocks & Minerals

A Rock is a naturally occurring solid aggregate of one or more minerals or mineraloids. Three major groups of rocks are defined : (I) Igneous, (S) Sedimentary and (M) Metamorphic.

A Mineral is a naturally occurring substance that is solid and stable at room temperature, representable by a chemical formula, usually abiogenic, and has an ordered atomic structure.

1. Basalt (I)
2. Granite (I)
3. Pumice (I)
4. Gneiss (M)
5. Marble (M)
6. Quartzite (M)
7. Serpentine (M)
8. Bituminous Coal (S)
9. Lime Stone (S)
10. Sand Stone (S)
11. Agate
12. Calcite
13. Dolomite
14. Feldspar
15. Graphite
16. Gypsum
17. Magnetite
18. Pyrophillite
19. Quartz
20. Tourmaline

Jordanian Sandstone

Quartz

Iron ore

Images courtesy Raghav Venkat Iyer.

Chapter XII

Soil Conservation

India is primarily an agricultural country. The farmer provides food to over 1.3 billion people. Yet he is beset with countless problems such as untimely rains, floods, drought, lack of fertilizers, small land holdings, lack of cultivation advance to till his land, marketability of their produce etc. Most tenant farmers hold small plots of land, follow old traditional methods of agriculture and do not follow scientific methods of agriculture.

Most under-developed countries are facing hunger due to food shortage, uncontrolled population, soil infertility, climate devastation such as lack of rain or excessive rains or expanding deserts.

About few decades back, when we took a train or bus journey, to say Guntur, we used to see green agricultural fields. Today we see concrete jungles of high-rise buildings. These building are no doubt needed for industrial, commercial or residential purpose. But expansion of limits of human habitation has led to encroachment of lands, canals, lakes and reserved forest lands. Encounters between humans and wild animals in residential areas is on the rise, as these animals have been driven out of their habitat, the forest lands. Hence the available cultivable land and production of food crops is reducing.

Soil conservation is the urgent need of the hour. Soil provides nutrients essential for the growth of plants, animals and microorganisms. If the soil becomes unhealthy or polluted, the life cycle stops. Conservation is carried out to prevent loss of the topmost fertile layer of the soil. It protects natural resources, and restores habitats for plants, wild animals and organisms. This increases the quality and quantity of crop yield, whatever the farmer chooses to grow. Soil conservation is to maintain fertility. Soil conservation involves the following two steps:

1. To protect the soil from degradation, i.e., returning all organisms back to the soil.
2. To treat soil as a living ecosystem.

Soil is the home of living organisms that provides fertility to soil and hence good crops and a natural habitat for living organisms: They are several methods to protect soil fertility.

To preserve fertility of the topmost layer of the soil, we should avoid overuse of chemical fertilizers.

It is necessary to take the steps to increase the crop yield by adopting appropriate methods as it would otherwise hampers survival of plants and living organisms.

Changing the crops like rice, wheat, millets, if feasible and profitable may be desirable.

Increasing organic manures instead of excessive chemical fertilizers is preferable.

Like in the olden days, every house should try to grow in-house or roof top vegetables, flowers, fruits and prevent soil erosion by adopting rain water harvesting and storing organic waste.

Acknowledgements

My young teenage granddaughters, Pooja Siri and Nidhi Siri Gundimeda, studying in Chicago, USA came with their parents to India for a vacation. They started quizzing me about geology, the subject I had studied way back in 1951, and had admittedly forgotten about minerals, rock samples, and their composition. As they were quite curious, I ensured they visited the Research & Development Laboratories museum, National Mineral Development Corporation Ltd. Hyderabad. They were fascinated by the colors, texture of different minerals and rocks, methods of identifying them, know their uses etc. I was happy to see their interest in my work and the workplace.

My son, Madhukar Gundimeda, then suggested to me to write an elementary geology book helpful for children and youngsters. I used the covid epidemic period to keep myself busy writing this book primarily valuable to answer children's questions.

I also included useful information required for undergraduate students of Geology from the textbooks studied long back.

In the meantime, unfortunately, I lost my beloved wife, Gundimeda Radha Devi, due to ill health. I then tried to keep busy and completed this book, entitled "ELEMENTARY GEOLOGY FOR CHILDREN."

The intent is to generate interest in the field of geology, in today's young generation in the computer age.

My daughter, Dr. Nadimpally Sandhya Devi edited the book to make it interesting, simple with clarity omitting details. I also acknowledge the suggestions and encouragement from my sons, Madhukar and Ravi Gundimeda, my son-in-law, Nadimpally Venkata Ramana and other family members to publish the book without hesitation.

Raghav Venkat Iyer, a young 8th class student, from Aga Khan Academy and my daughter's neighbor's son, has a passion for collecting rocks. I acknowledge his spontaneous contribution of the beautiful images of rocks with names for this book making it more colorful, informative and interesting. He has personally taken the photographs and identified the rocks.

I acknowledge my young friends in R & D Laboratories, NMDC Ltd, Hyderabad, for enabling me to publish this book.

Annexure: 1

India's mineral production in March 2021

source: Ministry of Mines (kbr infographics)

Mineral (units)	Production in September 2021	Utilized in sept. 2021	Growth in sept.2021 over sept 2020 %	Production in March 2021	Utilized in March 2021	Change in March 2021 over March 2020 (base 2011-12: 100%)
Bauxite (thousand tonnes)	1436		-9.2		2,103	+33.4%
Chromite (thousand tonnes)	144		152.4	601		+45.8%
Crude petroleum (lakh tonnes)	24		-1.8	26		-3.1%
Coal (lakh tonnes)	518		8.3	960		+0.2%
Copper concentrate (thousand tonnes)	9			11		+50.2%
Diamond (carat)	51		-93.3	34		-98.9%
Gold (kilo gram)	116		11.5	148		-2.6%
Iron ore (lakh tonnes)	153		3.4	227		+13.7%

Lead concentrate (thousand tonnes)	31			41		+74.9%
Lignite (lakh tonnes)	35		48	52		+25.3%
Limestone (lakh tonnes)	292			391		+45.6%
Magnesite (thousand tonnes)	11		66.8	12		+44.9%
Manganese ore (thousand tonnes)	169			331		+80.1%
Natural gas (million cu.m		2840			2612	+12.2%
Phosphate (thousand tonnes)	80		-40.4	124		+57%
Zinc concentrate (thousand tonnes)	133			164		+43.2%
Petroleum crude (lakh tonnes)	24					
	As per ministry of mines 18/11/2021					

Annexure: 2

sale price of iron ores of NMDC Ltd in Rs/tonne

Mineral/ ore	Company	+10mm lumps	-10mm fines	Remarks
Iron ore	NMDC Ltd	6150	5160	Bse filing; effective 4/9/21

Annexure: 3

Index of minerals

Magnesium ore/magnesite	53
Magnetite ore	61
Manganese ore	49
Marble	59
Mercury ore	56
Molybdenum ore	52
Monazite	67
Muscovite mica	80
Nickel minerals	41
Petroleum crude/naphtha	73
Pitch blende/uraninite	66
Platinum	31
Pyroxene family/augite	79
Quartz	76
Radium	67
Silicates mineral family	74
Silver	25
Sulphur	58
Uranium (radium)	65
Talc	79
Tin mineral/cassiterite	41
Titanium ore minerals/rutile/ilmenite	47
Topaz	33
Tourmaline mineral	34
Tungsten minerals/wolframite/scheelite	44
Vanadium mineral	51
Zinc minerals/sphalerite	38
Zircon	86

Annexure: 4

References

S.no.	Topic/name of author/name of publisher
1	Arthur Holmes; principles of physical geology; Thomas Nelson & sons ltd
2	Textbook of physics & chemistry; 39th edition
3	Routley's elements of mineralogy; twenty-sixth edition; Thomas Murry & co
4	Dennis W.H; metallurgy of nonferrous metals; Sir Isaac pitman & sons; London; 1954
5	Geological survey bulletin 914; microscopic determination of the ore minerals; united states department of the interior; second edition; united states government printing office; 1940
6	Alton wade. F and Richard b. Mattox; elements of crystallography and mineralogy; oxford & ibh publishing co., New Delhi; January 1960
7	Wahlstrom e. Ernest; optical crystallography; II Nd edition; john Wiley & sons Inc.; New York;
8	Petrographic mineralogy, Wahlstrom e. Ernest; John Wiley & sons, Chapman & Hall Ltd, London

www.ingramcontent.com/pod-product-compliance
Ingram Content Group UK Ltd.
Pitfield, Milton Keynes, MK11 3LW, UK
UKHW062256290726
14090UKWH00017B/720